Victorian Photo Memes

Written and designed by Rob Ward

© 2018 Studio Press
An imprint of Kings Road Publishing.
Part of Bonnier Publishing
The Plaza, 535 King's Road, London, SW10 0SZ

www.bonnierpublishing.co.uk

Printed in China

2 4 6 8 10 9 7 5 3 2 1

Victorian Photo Memes

Written by Rob Ward

When you find out you've got to get the replacement bus service to work.

When your mate is there to console you when you flip your ride the day after you pass your driving test.

When the bride makes sure she won't get shown up at her wedding with her choice of bridesmaids' dresses.

When you realise that your Super Daily Saver ticket wasn't such a great deal after all.

*When your teacher tells you art
is being replaced with double maths.*

When you try to convince a girl you're a lot older than you actually are with your 'authentic' facial hair.

*When you are desperate to get
your children to eat their five-a-day.*

When you impress your mates with your very realistic 'ostrich riding' costume.

When your work squad see you being picked up after your shift by a new guy.

When you've had a few drinks and your confidence levels surpass everyone's expectations.

When your last passport photo was rejected because you were smiling.

When your mum suddenly reveals that the eggs she used in the brownies were four weeks out of date.

When you try to make it incredibly obvious you'd like service at your table but are too polite to shout.

When word gets out that you're a designated driver at the office Christmas party.

When you stand still for a moment and start to blend in with the soft furnishings.

When you're forced to look at your parents' holiday photos.

When your wife actually heard you muttering grumpily about her under your breath.

When you and your mates forget it's non-school uniform day but try to make the most of it anyway.

When you blow the rest of the competition out of the water at the Year One talent show.

When you try to persuade people
you don't have a drinking problem by
showing them you only use a small glass.

When you come back from a two-week holiday and wish you'd cut the grass before you left.

When you are denied access to the cinema because they think you are two school kids trying to sneak in.

When you knock your host's garden statue over but try to act as though nothing has happened.

When you're really bored so you check your heart rate to make sure you're not flatlining.

*When you boast about how the hat
you have at home is even taller.*

When you get to the end of putting your flat-pack dining set together and it becomes apparent you've not quite followed the instructions correctly.

When you notice someone's label sticking out and fight the urge to tuck it back in.

When you discover a great way to get that little bit of food out from between your teeth.

When you try to blame the smell on the baby.

When you see what's on Saturday night TV
and remember what it used to be like.

When you may have taken your DIY '70s synth keyboard set-up too far.

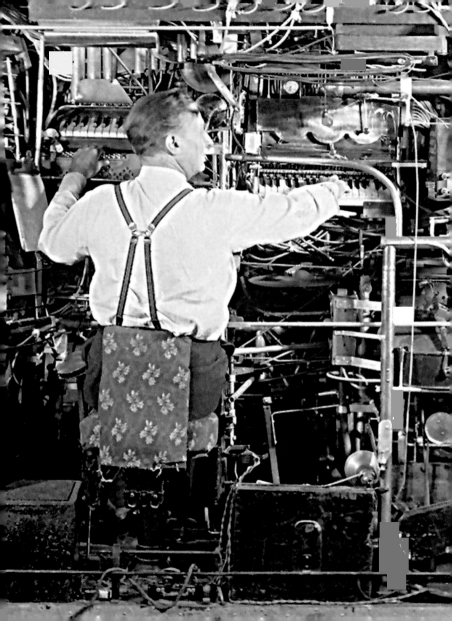

When you aren't quite as keen on theme parks as your mates.

When you've tried to artificially raise your heart rate in order to get out of triple science.

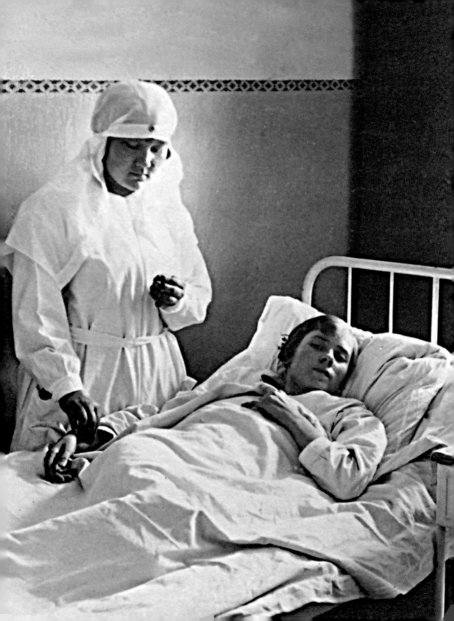

When the girl you like sends you a pic, but you can't find anywhere your stupid phone can get 4G.

When kids are making noise in the library,
but your wife suggests that you 'leave it'.

*When you're presented with your
'Employee of the Month' prize but think
your boss might have had a sneaky taster.*

When you get your drinks mixed up and you're both conviced you've drunk the least.

When your mum insists you and your twin brother still wear matching clothes because it's 'cute'.

When you carefully approach your wife to ask whether it's OK for you to go and meet your mates at the pub.

When you vow that it'll be the last time you choose a horse for the Grand National based on the name alone.

When you try and act chill next to your ride in the hope that everyone will notice your new rims.

When someone makes a ridiculously stupid guess for your award-worthy charade.

When you and your mate just couldn't resist
a good 'buy one get one half price' deal.

When you devise a cunning plan and convince him to carry you for the rest of the walk.

When you try and dissociate yourself from your embarrassing husband in your Mexico holiday photos.

When your mate says 'Don't worry he won't bite.'

*When your dad forgets to get you a birthday present,
so you march him down the shops immediately.*

When you realise that the fresh paint on the bench hadn't quite dried.

When your date invites you back to his place, but you are regretting how quickly you ate your pudding.

*When you walk through the front gate
and remember you've left your keys at work.*

When you ordered your pizza 29 minutes ago and you're debating whether you should leave it another minute before calling them.

When you turn up to your date's house with flowers and chocolates, only to find she's on a diet and suffering from hayfever.

When your bout of man-flu is so bad, the doc might as well pronounce a time of death.

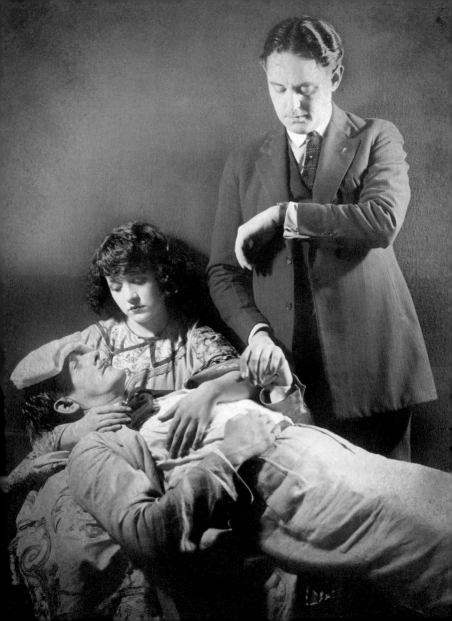

When you give in to your child's demands
and decorate the tree with Cheerios™.

When your wife agrees you'll both go and visit her parents for the weekend without asking you.

When you try to weigh up whether or not it would just be easier to buy a new hat.

When you get to the front of the airport queue and realise your passport is right at the bottom of your case.

When the plug socket in your hotel room is too far from the bed.

*When the guy in front of you at the
checkout has more than 10 items.*

*When your girl confirms who's boss
by reminding you that she can exact her revenge with
an accurate forehand, low and down the middle.*

When you answer your phone and it's someone trying to persuade you that you've been in an accident.

When you've caught up with a live TV programme,
so can no longer fast-forward through the adverts.

When you pretend not to be reading a whole novel in the bookshop as the sales assistant walks past.

When you luck out and get to ride the lion on the carousel at the fair.

When you get in a bit of a muddle trying to light all the candles on your grandma's birthday cake.

When you show off your latest idea for beating the rush hour traffic.

When you try and pretend you're close to working out a question on 'University Challenge', but your wife isn't falling for it.

When the size of the fish you're going
to catch increases by the second.

When you try to convince your wife that you were actually reading an interesting article on page FOUR of the newspaper.

When you don't quite trust your wife enough with your new car to actually let her drive with the engine running.